Gossip

Deal with it
before word
gets around

Catherine Rondina • Illustrated by Dan Workman

James Lorimer & Company Ltd., Publishers
Toronto

You're checking your email one afternoon,

and you see there's a group message from someone at school. The subject line promises the dirt on someone in your class. *Cool!* you think, *Juicy gossip.* You begin to read the message, and become horrified as you realize that it's about *you!*

Surprise — you've just become the subject of gossip.

That's the way it works. First you're talking about someone then they're talking about you.

You've probably heard rumours or even spread gossip yourself. Everyone does it — parents do it, teachers, too. Gossip about celebrities is a multi-million-dollar business. Sometimes we talk about people because we care or are concerned about them, and sometimes we just want to share a good story. But what usually begins as a small rumour can get bigger and bigger until it becomes something totally different from the truth.

So what's the big deal?

Words can hurt, and we all care about what other people think of us. The stories spread by gossiping can be just as painful as a physical blow. If you are being gossiped about, you might feel scared, alone, and unhappy. You may feel that everyone is talking behind your back, and worry that everyone believes the rumours. And you probably feel helpless to stop the rumours.

It can be hard to avoid gossip when you hear it all around you. So how can you stop it from spreading? That's where this book comes in — it can help you see the difference between sharing information and gossiping, and it can show you how to deal with gossip before it gets out of control.

Contents

Everyone talks about other people, right?

Real gossiping is when a group of kids gets together to dig up and spread nasty information about the new girl at school. Well sure, everyone knows that people are gossipers. But gossip can also get started anytime a person...

Criticizes people behind
their backs

Makes up a story
about someone

Guesses something might happen
and tells people it already has

Reveals personal
information about
someone

Shares someone's personal
thoughts or feelings with
others

Says something about someone
to get attention

Lies about someone

Tells someone's secret

And gossip doesn't stop there, or it wouldn't be gossip. It needs more people to...

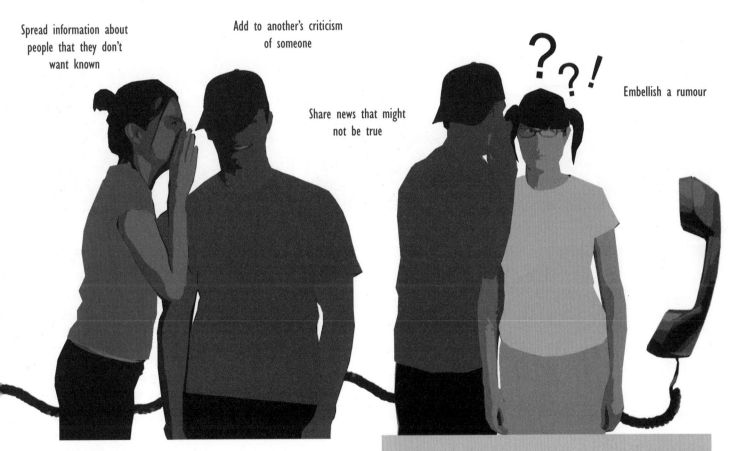

Indulge in "juicy" or personal talk about people

Spread information about people that they don't want known

Add to another's criticism of someone

Forward an email with personal information about someone

Talk behind a person's back

Share news that might not be true

Embellish a rumour

Whenever private or negative things are discussed behind someone's back, it's gossip. It doesn't matter whether the information is true or false, whether you start the rumour or just keep it going, if it doesn't stop its travels with you, you're gossiping.

SPECULATION

AMY SEES JAKE LEAVING THE SCHOOL WITH HIS FATHER

THAT NIGHT...

Jake's dad was at school and Jake didn't look very happy.

ONLINE...

JAKE GOT IN TROUBLE AT SCHOOL, AND HIS DAD CAME TO GET HIM BECAUSE HE WAS SUSPENDED.

SEND

Word gets around . . .

SECRETS

Are you okay?

My parents are getting a divorce. Please don't tell anyone.

...but please don't tell anyone.

AT THE MALL...

SLANDER

Yeah, let's start a rumour!

Let's teach Brenda a lesson.

Hey girls, guess what?

I heard that Brenda got caught stealing an MP3 player!

INSINUATION

Thanks, but let's just be friends.

Would you like to go out sometime?

He doesn't like you?

What's wrong with him?

Hmm...

Sorry you got suspended buddy

I wasn't suspended. I was in Vancouver.

A FEW DAYS LATER...

You told people I was suspended?

Then why was your Dad at school?

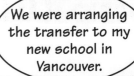

We were arranging the transfer to my new school in Vancouver.

How could you tell everyone?! You're no friend of mine.

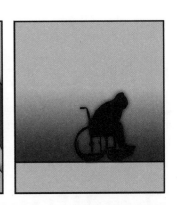

WHISPER
WHISPER
WHISPER

She's going to have a criminal record and everything.

Where are these lies coming from?

WHISPER
WHISPER
WHISPER

If he turned HER down we know what THAT must mean...

LATER THAT WEEK...

I thought we were friends. Why didn't you tell me you were gay?

FAG

QUIZ

Is it gossiping or not? What if you are concerned about a friend, and want to talk it over with someone? It can be confusing. Keep this in mind: it's gossiping if the story or information is 1) private, 2) possibly untrue, 3) hurtful or embarrassing for someone. Read through the examples below and decide if you think the kids involved are gossiping or not.

TROUBLE AT HOME

1 Sean and Jacob are best friends. Jacob tells Sean that, ever since his father lost his job, all his dad does is sit around all day and get angry at everyone.

Shoplifting Shock

2 One day after school Eric sees Kareem at the convenience store. Eric thinks he sees Kareem put something in his pocket and leave the store without paying. That night at dinner Eric tells his mom and dad.

Lousy Lice

3 Carla and Alex have never liked Kristina. They start a rumour that Kristina has lice in her hair. Before long, everyone at school is avoiding Kristina and whispering that if you get too close to her, you'll get bugs too.

Soccer Stance

4 Jenny and Samantha met at soccer practice and became good friends. But once the soccer season ended, Jenny didn't want anything to do with Samantha. Samantha wasn't sure why their friendship ended, until a mutual friend told her that Jenny said she was a ball hog and didn't have any team spirit.

Sleezy Rumour

5 All the boys in class are talking about how Pam will fool around with anyone. Pam's friend Keri tells Paul that Pam wonders why none of the nice boys will ask her out, so he lets her in on the rumours.

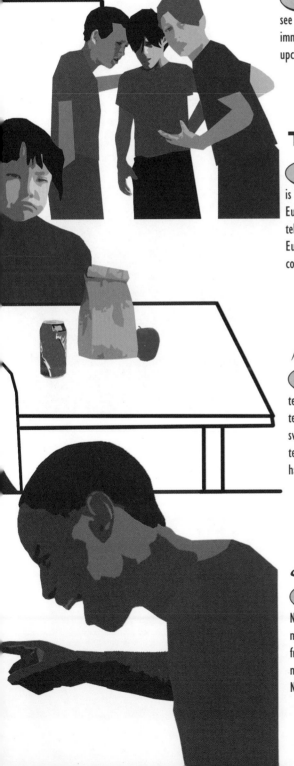

Artful Dreams

6 Desmond loves to play basketball and the coach says he's the best player in the league. What Desmond really wants to do is be an artist, and he tells Kyle that one day he hopes to be a great painter. Kyle tells all the guys on the team about Desmond's dreams.

DATING DELIGHT

7 Darcy calls up Jackie and asks her to go see a movie with him. She says yes and immediately e-mails all her girlfriends about the upcoming date.

Teaching Trauma

8 Mr. Monarch tells his grade 3 class he is taking a year away from teaching to travel in Europe. Some of the kids misunderstand him and tell their parents that he is leaving to teach in Europe because he can't find a job in the community.

FAMILY MATTERS

9 Emma overhears her older sister Liz telling their parents that she is a lesbian. Emma tells her best friend Rachael, and makes Rachael swear that she won't tell anyone. But Rachael does tell. When Liz gets to school the next day someone has written a horrible message on her locker.

Smoking Secrets

10 Sarah discovers that her friend Naoko is smoking, and tells her own mother. Sarah and Naoko's mothers are friends, and Sarah's mother tells Naoko's mother that her daughter is smoking. Naoko gets in big trouble.

Answers

1. No: Jacob has confided in Sean because he is his best friend. Jacob is not gossiping about his father, he's just talking about a problem his family is experiencing.

2. No: Eric wasn't sure he saw Kareem stealing, but felt that he needed to tell someone. In telling his parents, instead of friends, he can be pretty sure the rumour won't spread.

3. Yes: Carla and Alex intentionally made up a lie and started a nasty rumour about Kristina to hurt her.

4. Yes: No matter why Jenny ended the friendship, when she told someone else that Samantha wasn't a fair player she was saying things behind her back.

5. No: Although the boys **are** gossiping about Pam, Keri is not; she's trying to help her friend find out what is going on. Paul is not gossiping about Pam because he knows Keri will tell Pam.

6. Yes: When Desmond told Kyle his dreams of becoming an artist and not playing basketball, it was a personal conversation between Desmond and Kyle, and Kyle should have kept this information to himself.

7. No: Jackie is not gossiping by telling her friends about her date with Darcy. This is news about her and she has every right to tell her friends about it.

8. No: The kids are giving false information to their parents, but not on purpose. It would be gossip only if the parents then spread the false information any further.

9. Yes: Ok for Emma to talk to friend. Rachael should have keep her promise not to tell anyone else.

10. No: Sarah wasn't trying to get Naoko in trouble. She was worried about Naoko and knew that smoking was bad for her. Naoko might think that the information was private, but Sarah told her mom because she didn't know what to do to help her friend.

Myths

IF YOU TELL THE TRUTH IT ISN'T GOSSIPING

Even when the information you are spreading is true,
it's still gossiping if the information is private or personal.

You can't **HURT** someone with **WORDS**

Words can hurt just as much as being hit or punched. When you spread rumours or gossip about someone, you are definitely hurting them.

DID YOU KNOW?

- Slander is a rumour that is spread in order to cause trouble and disgrace someone.

A Gossiper is someone "IN THE KNOW"

Actually, people who gossip all the time make up a lot of the rumours that they spread. They may have become gossipers because of their need for attention.

It's not gossip if it's **written down**

Gossip can be spread in many different ways. It doesn't matter if it's online, in notes sent to people, or even published.

GIRLS GOSSIP, not boys

While statistics show that girls gossip more than boys, that doesn't mean boys don't love a good rumour. Boys usually don't start gossip, but they are often involved in spreading it.

- People often use slander as a means of revenge.
- Libel is slander in written form.
- Celebrities often sue newspapers for defamation.
- Often rumours start when people simply get information wrong.

Dear Gossip Counsellor

Q. Last week someone slashed the tires of six bikes that were chained to the schoolyard fence. During announcements, our principal asked anyone who saw anything to come to her office. I saw who slashed the bike tires, but if I tell the principal, is that gossiping?

— Afraid to Tell

A. Sometimes it's difficult to have to tell the truth — but telling the principal what you saw is not gossiping. You should speak to her as soon as possible and let her deal with the kids who damaged the bikes. It's not gossiping when you are telling the truth about a serious situation to someone who deserves to know.

Q. My best friend Tia is really a great person — most of the time. But whenever I tell her about something personal, she always tells her other friend Shirley. I like Shirley, but I don't want her knowing all my personal business. Is it gossiping if Shirley is the only one Tia tells? — *Tired of Tia Talking*

A. Yes, Tia is gossiping about you to Shirley. She may not mean any harm, but by telling Shirley things that you meant to share only with her, Tia is spreading information that isn't Shirley's business. The best way to put a stop to this is to tell Tia that you don't like it. Explain to her that some things you tell her are private and for her ears only.

Q. This girl at my school is always following me around. Recently she told someone that I asked her out and she said no. I don't really care if she likes me or not, but I don't like her spreading lies about me asking her out. How do I stop her! — *Not Dating*

A. This girl seems to have a bit of a crush on you, but she's going about it all the wrong way. By spreading false rumours about you and her, she's definitely gossiping. Confront her about the rumour and tell her you'd appreciate it if she didn't make up stories about the two of you.

Q. In January, my friend Cindy phoned me to say that her dad said there was a big snowstorm coming and school would probably be cancelled the next day. I e-mailed a bunch of my friends and told them we wouldn't have school, so we decided not to finish our homework. Guess what! School was open the next day and all my friends got angry with me. It wasn't my fault. I only told them what I heard, right? — *Snow Story*

A. Each of your friends made his or her own decision about not doing homework, but you still should not have spread the story about school being cancelled. You were giving out information you didn't know was true. Next time check the facts first before you hit "send".

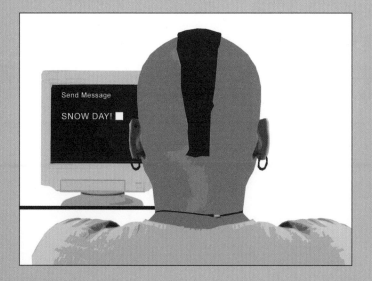

So, you're the biggest grape on the grapevine, eh?

You love to be the first to know all the important info. When you hear something really juicy about someone, even if you're not sure it's true, you itch to tell someone else. There's no harm in a little chitchat between friends, right? You'd never hurt anybody — would you?

DEAR DR. SHRINK-WRAPPED . . .

Q: There's this group of girls on my soccer team who love to gossip about everything and everybody. They're constantly huddled in a little circle gabbing about someone. Our coach calls them the Gossip Girls, and she's always asking them to stop talking and pay attention to the game. I don't usually like to gossip, but it looks like fun. I want to be a Gossip Girl, too. Is there anything wrong with that?

— Gossip Groupie

spreading rumours, you might do the same thing to fit in. When you're "in on the secret" you're officially in the group.

- For excitement — Sometimes life may seem a little dull or boring, so people decide to spice things up by spreading juicy stories. That's actually what tabloid newspapers and celebrity TV shows do: they make the celebrities' lives look more exciting by spreading rumours.

A: Dr. Shrink-Wrapped understands that you want to join your teammates in their fun. But you have to think about why they use gossip as a way of grouping together, and why you want to start gossiping to be with them. There are a number of reasons people gossip — here are a few examples:

- To feel better about yourself — If you're feeling bad about yourself, it's pretty common to want someone else to feel worse off than you do. The easiest way to do that is to spread rumours about someone and make them feel lousy too.

- To get attention — Gossiping can make you feel important, and put you at the centre of attention, because you know something no one else does. Everyone pays attention to the first person to find out something, or to share a hot piece of gossip.

- To feel like part of a group — Sometimes all you want to do is belong in a group, so if everyone is gossiping and

Q: My best friend, Haley, is really mad at me. She entered this art contest and won first prize! I wanted to tell all our friends, but she asked me not to say anything just yet. Now she's mad at me for telling a few people that she won. I don't get it. What's wrong with spreading good news?

— Bearer of Good News

A: Dr. Shrink-Wrapped knows that it can be hard not to share a secret, especially when it's good news. But if your friend Haley asked you not to tell anyone about her winning the art contest, she must have had a reason. You think that you're doing her a favour by telling your pals about her success, but if you spread the news around about her against her wishes, then you're gossiping — and you've betrayed her trust. In the future keep your friend's secrets to yourself, and you'll be a better friend for it.

The **Gossiper**

QUIZ

Do you love to dish the dirt about everyone? So when exactly does a fascinating conversation turn into hurtful gossip? Take this quiz and see what you can find out. Of the following statements, how many are true, and how many are false?

Are you a gossip hound?

1 I tell great stories about other people.

2 My friends always come to me first to find out what's going on.

3 I think everyone deserves to know about the people around them.

4 If you don't want to be talked about, you should never do anything wrong.

5 It doesn't matter if it's true or false, as long as it's interesting.

6 If someone tells me something, they expect everyone to find out.

7 I don't believe people should keep secrets.

8 I've lost friends because I told their personal information to others.

9 The goal of journalism is to dig for the dirtiest secrets.

10 I have told "fibs" about others to make myself look better.

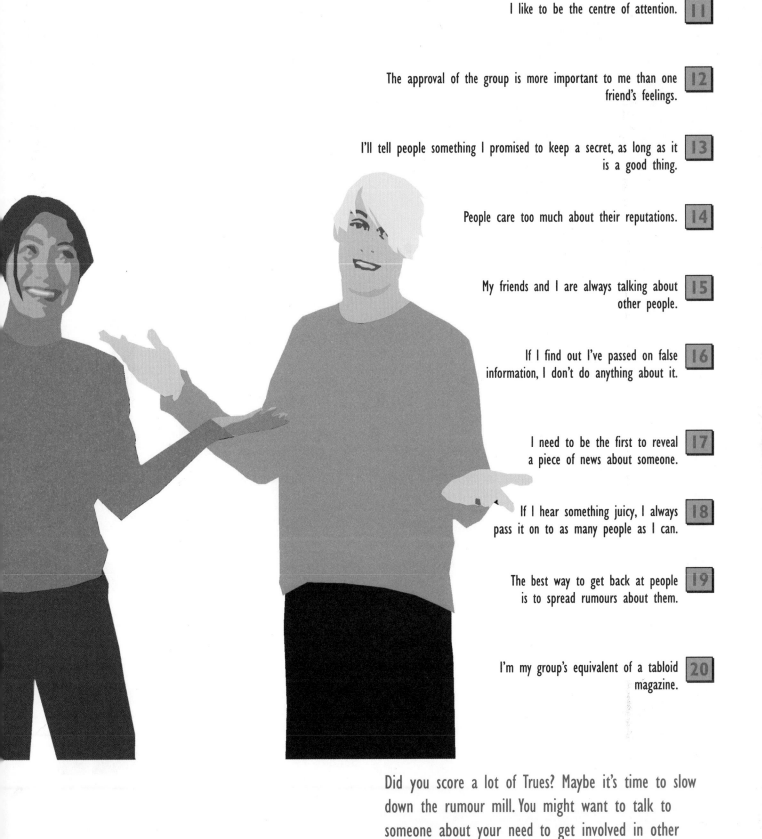

I like to be the centre of attention. `11`

The approval of the group is more important to me than one friend's feelings. `12`

I'll tell people something I promised to keep a secret, as long as it is a good thing. `13`

People care too much about their reputations. `14`

My friends and I are always talking about other people. `15`

If I find out I've passed on false information, I don't do anything about it. `16`

I need to be the first to reveal a piece of news about someone. `17`

If I hear something juicy, I always pass it on to as many people as I can. `18`

The best way to get back at people is to spread rumours about them. `19`

I'm my group's equivalent of a tabloid magazine. `20`

Did you score a lot of Trues? Maybe it's time to slow down the rumour mill. You might want to talk to someone about your need to get involved in other people's business.

The **Gossiper**

Hey, gossip can be a really nasty thing. If you go around telling stories that you're not sure are true, sooner or later no one will believer anything you tell them! (Remember the story of the boy who cried wolf?) Once your friends realize they can't trust you to keep a secret, they'll never tell you anything personal again. Before long, you won't have friends left to gossip about.

You can't really stop other people from gossiping, but you can break the gossip chain. Here are some steps to take if you want to be a gossip buster.

Avoid kids who like to gossip. If you can stay clear of the crowd whose favourite pastime is talking about others, they'll soon get the idea that you're not interested in their silly tattling.

How to Stop the Gossip

Think before you speak. You've heard a rumour about someone you know. Before you pass it on, think about what is being said and why. Use the 5W's formula:

• Who is this information going to harm?

• What is the reason behind all this dishing?

• Will spreading this rumour hurt someone else?

• Why would I want to pass this information on?

• Would this person be hurt if they knew what was being said about them?

Put a stop to the rumour. If you hear a rumour that is hurtful in some way, don't repeat it. You can take a stand by refusing to pass on harmful gossip about

someone. Stamp out gossip with your feet — just walk away!

Value the privacy of others. If you don't want other people to talk about you and your personal life, then don't talk about the personal lives of others. Keep in mind that if you respect people's privacy, they're more likely to respect yours.

Hear no evil. When someone hooks you up with some gossip that is mean or harmful, don't listen to what they're saying. Chances are, they want you to help spread their nasty rumour in order to hurt someone else, or they're trying to get attention.

Be a gossip buster. If you feel that your friends are spreading gossip that could hurt someone, tell them you think it's wrong. Stand up to gossip bullies who use words to try and harm others.

do's and don'ts

✓ Do keep a secret when you're told one.

✓ Do try to stop a rumour when it gets to you.

✓ Do realize how harmful gossip can be.

✓ Do tell a friend if you hear a rumour is being spread about them.

✓ Do think before you talk about someone else.

✗ Don't reveal someone's personal or private information.

✗ Don't gossip just to fit in.

✗ Don't get involved in a group that spends all its time gossiping.

✗ Don't become a gossip bully.

✗ Don't say things behind someone's back.

✗ Don't believe everything you hear.

✗ Don't let gossip cost you a friendship.

---

threatening and often quickly forgotten.

• An "urban myth" is a sensational tale about modern life.

• Urban myths are repeated in the media and on the Internet, making the story more believable to some.

Let's face it,

when it comes to rumours and gossip, everyone's fair game. A lot of the time gossiping can seem like fun, then all of a sudden the situation changes and you're the one being talked about, the Subject of all that talk.

We've probably all been the subject of gossip at one time or another, and often it's just harmless chatter passed around to try to create some excitement. People have probably said things about you that you weren't even aware of. But when someone starts a rumour about you with the intention of causing harm, they're using gossip to bully you. It can be difficult to ignore gossip being spread about you, and even harder to pretend it doesn't hurt your feelings.

A gossiper usually picks a victim who is an easy target — someone they know others will be interested in chatting about — such as
• popular kids
• unpopular kids
• smart kids
• disadvantaged kids
• kids who are different in any way

Sometimes they even gossip about their own friends or choose an unknown victim at random, just to make themselves feel superior.

do's and don'ts

✓ Do talk to an adult if gossip is making your life miserable.

✓ Do be supportive of someone who is being gossiped about.

✓ Do try to ignore gossip when you hear it.

✓ Do tell your parents or a trustworthy adult if gossip is getting to you.

✓ Do remember to turn the other cheek when someone gossips about you.

✓ Do keep in mind that people often gossip just to make themselves feel better because they're unhappy or insecure.

✓ Do realize that you may be a victim right now, but a gossip bully will probably be picking on someone else next week.

✗ Don't let gossiping get to you — you didn't do anything wrong.

✗ Don't hang out with people who like to gossip.

✗ Don't spread rumours yourself.

✗ Don't be afraid to confront a gossip and ask them to stop spreading lies about you.

✗ Don't blame yourself if people are gossiping about you. It's their problem, not yours.

✗ Don't let a gossip bully see that they've upset you.

✗ Don't resort to using revenge when people gossip about you.

HIGH RD.

21

DEAR DR. SHRINK-WRAPPED...

Q. I'm always being gossiped about at school. No matter what I do, people tell all kinds of lies about me. It's gotten to the point where I don't like to go to school because it seems like everyone is always whispering about me behind my back. Why can't I take it? Am I as pathetic as they all say?
— *Being Ground in the Rumour Mill*

A. Take it from Dr. Shrink-Wrapped — you're not pathetic, and all those gossipers are wrong about you! If they were on the receiving end of the rumours, they'd be just as hurt. When people spread gossip it can be very hurtful because it is usually a personal attack. Saying negative things, telling stories that you're not sure are true, or revealing personal information is a betrayal of friendship and of basic respect — that's why it hurts so much. Here are some examples of why gossip and rumours can really hurt:

Gossip is as bad as physical bullying
Words can hurt a person just as much as a punch, and sometimes the damage lasts much longer. Remember, "sticks and stones may break my bones" – but words can also really hurt.

Gossip can be used to exclude others
Many bullies use gossip as a way of excluding kids they don't like. When you spread a rumour about someone, you're telling others that the subject of your gossip is not part of your group, and it's okay to make fun of him or her. It's a social bully's way of making someone feel like an outsider.

Gossip can destroy friendships and trust
People who like to spread rumours often do it to attract people to them. Ironically, they may soon find that they don't have as many real friends as they used to. When friends realize a gossiper can't be trusted not to gossip about them, the secrets dry up.

Gossip can get you into trouble
You've probably heard the saying "Don't believe everything you hear." That goes double for gossip. Most gossip is either made up or misinterpreted. Use your good judgment when you hear gossip, and don't be easily influenced by those who whisper behind other people's backs.

When Technology is Involved

Have you ever wondered how gossip first got started? People have probably been dishing about each other for as long as humans have been able to speak! As forms of communication become more advanced, the spread of gossip has become faster and reaches farther. With today's technology people can spread rumours almost as quickly as they can talk or type. Think about it: if you live in Halifax and you want to get the word out fast to friends in Vancouver, how could you do it?

- Over the telephone?

- On your cell phone?

- By email?

- Through text-messaging?

- In a chat room?

- On a web page?

E-gossip
In fact, we don't even need to use words to gossip these days. You can scan a photograph, or take a picture with your digital camera, and circulate it by email. Or you could snap a shot with a cell phone camera and send it instantly to whomever you want.

Words can hurt
Because the Internet is so powerful, it's important to use it responsibly. Think about how often someone in your chat group gossips or makes negative comments about others. You feel more anonymous when you're typing, rather than talking to people face to face. But just because you're not dissing someone out loud, doesn't mean you're not causing harm. No matter what form gossip takes, it can still hurt someone.

Be web wise
Always keep your wits about you when you receive information through email or the Internet. This is especially important when you get SPAM (that's email you didn't want or from someone you don't know). Be very careful about believing what you read! SPAM is often totally fake. Lots of smart people have passed around phony news stories, signed bogus petitions, and even sent their money to scam artists because of hoaxes spread by SPAM. Never give out your personal information or buy something through the Internet without checking with an adult first.

The **Subject**

There are some basic things you can do if you find yourself the subject of gossip.

Investigate the cause

Get to the source of the gossip and try to find out why people are gossiping about you. Is someone spreading gossip to hurt you or is it just a false rumour being passed around. Perhaps someone is trying to get back at you for something you said or did? Figuring out why the gossip is spreading is very important because once you know the reasons behind it you can deal with it and with those who are responsible for it.

Stay Cool

Don't let the bullying get to you. People who gossip love to see that their rumours upset their victims. Try not to let your feelings show. Remember that someone who starts a rumour that is meant to hurt someone else is probably doing it because they feel unhappy or insecure.

Don't Fight Fire with Fire

Never use revenge to solve a conflict. When someone is gossiping behind your back, it's hard not to not turn around and do the same thing back. You'd probably love to make up a rumour about the gossipers or tell a secret you know, just to get back at them. But in the end, it's not worth it — all you're doing is stooping to their level, and becoming a gossip bully too!

DID YOU KNOW?

- "Word-of-mouth" means information is spread through talking.

- A gossip columnist is a journalist who writes gossip about celebrities.

Protect your privacy
Keep personal information to yourself. The more you tell people private information about yourself, the greater the chance that your secrets will be used against you by the gossips. Be careful about who you entrust your secrets to.

Don't say it if you can't take it
If you don't want to be gossiped about, then it only makes sense not to gossip about others. You can't be a person who enjoys spreading rumours and then get upset if someone starts a rumour about you.

Keep good friends close
Your best defence is a best friend you can trust to be on your side. Having a loyal pal who watches out for you and lets you know if someone is gossiping about you can make all the difference. Remember to be a true friend in return, and treat your buddy with the same respect.

- A tabloid is a type of newspaper that features a lot of gossip about celebrities.
- Tabloids sometimes pay huge sums of money for photographs showing celebrities in their private lives.

When you get to school

a group of your pals is gathered together talking. You approach them and ask, "What's up?" Everyone starts saying how the new kid was just taken away in a police car. One girl says he was arrested. Another says he was stoned and crying. Someone else says they heard he had a knife.

Gossip is flying everywhere.

What to Believe?

You feel really confused. Do you believe all the wild stories you're hearing? Are you anxious to get to class and find out more about the kid? Or maybe you should get on your cell phone and start calling all your friends with the dirty details. You've just become a witness to gossip — now you have to decide what you are going to do about it.

It's Up to You

You can't stop the gossip from spreading, but it's your decision whether you participate in it. When you witness gossip, you have four options:
1. You can spread the stories you've heard and keep hyping the gossip.
2. You can tell your friends to stop gossiping until they know what really happened.
3. You can wait for the kid to return to school and get the facts straight from him.
4. You can choose not to listen to the gossip and rumours at all, whether they're true or not.

do's and don'ts

✓ Do tell an adult you can trust if you hear gossip that is harmful or dangerous.

✓ Do take a stand against spreading rumours.

✓ Do refuse to gossip about others.

✓ Do tell gossipers that you're not interested in their stories and lies.

✓ Do let a person being gossiped about know what is being said about them.

✓ Do let a gossip victim know you're their friend.

✓ Do challenge your friends when they gossip — let them know you're not interested in talking behind other people's backs.

✗ Don't let gossip ruin your friendships.

✗ Don't encourage gossip.

✗ Don't spread the gossip you've heard.

✗ Don't be afraid to talk with an adult if you've heard gossip that is scary or harmful.

✗ Don't let the gossiper bully you or bully the subject of the gossip.

QUIZ

Do you really get it?

You can see how damaging gossip can be to people, but do you really get it? What would you do in the following situations? This quiz has no right or wrong answers, because each situation is unique. Your answers may be different from the suggestions, but they could be right, under the circumstances.

Gay Gossip

1 While your friend Oscar is away over summer vacation, someone starts a rumour that he is gay. You hear the gossip going around. What should you do?

PREGNANT PAUSE

2 At the skate park, you overhear a girl tell her whole crowd that a girl named Shanti is pregnant. Shanti is the sister of your best friend. What should you do?

- Don't respond to the rumour. You don't know if it is true.
- Tell your friend that you don't mean to butt in, but a rumour is starting to get around about her sister and she may want to let her sister know about it.
- If you are friends with Shanti too, approach her tentatively, saying that you think she should know that people are talking about her.

- Tell Oscar about the rumour. Explain that you wanted to speak up for him, but were afraid that you might make matters worse.
- Try to brainstorm, with Oscar, a way to stop the rumours about him.
- Whether the rumour is true or not, talk to a teacher or guidance counsellor about tolerance-building measures that can be taken at your school.

SHINER STORY

3 Your friend comes to school one day with a black eye. When asked what happened, he says he walked into a door, but nobody believes him. Word is getting around that his father is beating his mother, and he got the black eye by stepping in. Some people are treating him like a hero, but he is very uncomfortable about the whole situation. What do you do?

- Tell anyone spreading the rumour that your friend's home life is none of their business.
- Even if you suspect it isn't true, support your friend's version of what happened.
- Ask your friend if you can do anything to help. Just knowing you are on his side will probably make him feel better.
- Offer to go with your friend to seek help from a guidance counsellor, teacher, or another trusted adult.

Smokin' Sue

4 Your friend Sue is really upset. Someone has been telling everyone that she does drugs. She is really freaked out and worried about what people will think about her. What do you do?

- If the rumour was started by someone with a grudge against Sue, try to let people know that they can't trust what the gossiper says.
- Offer to back Sue up if she decides to tell her parents. It would be better that Sue let them know about the gossip than if they heard from other people.
- Be a good friend. Every time someone tries to tell you the gossip, defend Sue and tell them that they shouldn't be spreading lies about people.

VANDAL SCANDAL

5 You overhear a conversation between two boys at your church group. They are laughing and talking about how they spray-painted and smashed windows in an old building downtown, but are spreading the rumour that it was done by some other kids. What do you do?

- If you know the kids being blamed for the vandalism, tell them that false information is being spread about them.
- Go to the head of the church group and tell what you heard.
- Ask an adult to go with you to tell the police. Vandalism is a crime.

Continues . . .

GRAFFITI GRIEF

6 You see a girl writing something nasty about a friend of yours on the bathroom walls and counters at school. What do you do?

- Confront the graffiti writer and ask why she is victimizing your friend.
- Warn the girl that you won't just sit by and let nasty things about your friend get spread by gossip.
- Report the graffiti to the school and offer to help paint over it.
- Stand by your friend. People will have a harder time believing nasty things about her if she has good friends like you.

MOVIE STUNT

7 Your best friend Cody dreams of being a professional stuntman one day. He's always telling you how he plans to run away to Hollywood to work on a movie set. One day, your friend Phil hears Cody's plans. Phil tells everyone, including Cody's dad, that your friend is thinking of running away. What do you do?

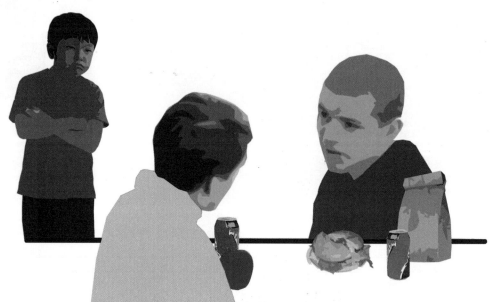

- Tell Phil that it was none of his business, and that Cody wasn't in any immediate danger.
- Apologize to Cody for Phil's actions.
- Offer to go with Cody to talk to his dad and clear things up.
- Find out why Phil took it upon himself to spread the rumour. He may be jealous of your friendship with Cody, and knowing that you understand why he did what he did will reassure him.

RELATIONSHIP RUMOURS

8 Jennifer and Tomas have been going out for five months. You hear through the grapevine that Jennifer wants to break up with Tomas. What do you do?

- Nothing. It is none of your business.
- If Tomas hears the gossip and comes to you for verification, tell him that it's just a rumour as far as you know.
- Suggest to Tomas that he have a serious talk with Jennifer to find out if there is any basis to the rumour.
- Tell whoever told you the rumour that they should not be gossiping.
- Try to find out who started the rumour. If it is someone with a grudge against Jennifer or Tomas, tell the gossipers that they should not trust that person's word.

Misconduct

9 You arrive at hockey practice to find the guys all talking about Naomi. They're all joking and laughing about a story Mark is telling about her. You know it's not true. What do you do?

- Ask Mark why he is spreading the rumour about Naomi.
- Quietly tell Naomi that rumours are being spread about her that aren't true.
- Tell your teammates that they shouldn't be spreading gossip about people.
- If the story is harmless, tell the guys they are being silly and ignore them.

IRKSOME INTERNET

10 Someone tells you that a nasty rumour is being spread about you through the Internet. They claim they can't say what the rumour is or who started it, but everyone knows your secret. What do you do?

- Ignore the e-mail. Many kinds of rumours are spread electronically, and not everyone believes them.
- Ask your friends if they have heard the rumour. Find out what is being said about you.
- Try to find out who started the rumour. It is easier to discredit gossip if you know how it got started.
- Remember how it feels, and promise yourself you will never spread gossip about others.

More Help

It takes time and practice to learn the skills in this book. There are many ways to deal with gossip, but only <u>you</u> know which feels right in each situation. In the end, the best strategy is the one that keeps gossip from hurting people.

If you need more information, or someone to talk to, the following Canadian resources may be of help:

Helplines

Kids Help Phone (Canada) 1-800-668-6868

Youth Crisis Hotline (USA) 1-800-448-4663

Web sites

It's My Life: http://pbskids.org/itsmylife/

KidsHealth: Kidshealth.org/kid/feeling

Kids Health Phone: http://kidshelp.sympatico.ca

Schoolnet.ca

Youthpath.ca

Books

Bad Boy by Diana Wieler. Groundwood Books, 1997.

Chanda's Secrets by Allan Stratton. Annick Press, 2004.

Great Lengths by Sandra Diersch. James Lorimer & Company, 1998.

For Sure! For Sure! by Hans Christian Andersen. Tradewind Books, 2004.

Lilly in the Middle by Brenda Bellingham. Formac Publishing, 2003.

Morgan's Secret by Ted Staunton. Formac Publishing, 2000.

A Noodle Up Your Nose by Frieda Wishinsky. Orca Book Publishers, 2004.

The Rumor: A Jataka Tale From India by Jan Thornhill. Maple Tree Press, 2002.

The Scream of the Hawk by Nancy Belgue. Orca Book Publishers, 2003.

Sticks and Stones by Beth Goobie. Orca Book Publishers, 2002.

Digging for Philip by Greg Jackson-Davis. Great Plains, 2003.

Other titles in the Deal With It series:

Arguing: Deal with it Word by Word by Elaine Slavens, illustrated by Steven Murray.

Bullying: Deal with it before Push comes to Shove by Elaine Slavens, illustrated by Brooke Kerrigan.

Competition: Deal with it from start to finish by Mireille Messier, illustrated by Steven Murray.

Fighting: Deal with it without coming to blows by Elaine Slavens, illustrated by Steven Murray.

Peer Pressure: Deal with it without losing your cool by Elaine Slavens, illustrated by Ben Shannon.

Racism: Deal with it Before It Gets Under Your Skin by Anne Marie Aikins, illustrated by Steven Murray.

Manufactured by Paramount Printing Company Limited in Tseung Kwan O, New Territories, Hong Kong in 2010.
Job Number: 130744

James Lorimer & Company Ltd. acknowledges the support of the Ontario Arts Council. We acknowledge the financial support of the Government of Canada through the Canada Book Fund for our publishing activities. We acknowledge the support of the Canada Council for the Arts for our publishing program. We acknowledge the support of the Government of Ontario through the Ontario Media Development Corporation's Ontario Book Initiative.

First published in the United States in 2011.

The Canada Council | Le Conseil des Arts
for the Arts | du Canada

ONTARIO ARTS COUNCIL
CONSEIL DES ARTS DE L'ONTARIO

Design: Blair Kerrigan/Glyphics

Library and Archives Canada Cataloguing in Publication

Rondina, Catherine
     Gossip : deal with it before word gets around / Catherine Rondina ; illustrated by Dan Workman.

(Deal with it)
ISBN 978-1-55277-499-1 (bound)
ISBN 978-1-55028-821-6 (pbk.)

     1. Gossip—Juvenile literature. I. Workman, Dan
II. Title. III. Series: Deal with it (Toronto, Ont.)

BJ1535.G6R66 2010   j177'.2   C2010-900278-4

James Lorimer & Company Ltd., Publishers
317 Adelaide Street West, Suite #1002
Toronto, Ontario
M5V 1P9
www.lorimer.ca

Distributed in the United States by:
Orca Book Publishers
P.O. Box 468
Custer, WA USA
98240-0468

Printed and bound in Hong Kong